Mezzo-Soprano/Belter V...
with Recorded Accompa...

MW00862024

THE
SINGERS
MUSICAL THEATRE
ANTHOLOGY

Compiled and Edited by Richard Walters

To access companion recorded accompaniments online, visit:
www.halleonard.com/mylibrary

Enter Code
4327-8676-7494-4529

ISBN 978-1-4234-2365-2

HAL•LEONARD®
CORPORATION
7777 W. BLUEMOUND RD. P.O. BOX 13819 MILWAUKEE, WI 53213

Visit Hal Leonard Online at
www.halleonard.com

Foreword
to the original edition

The Singer's Musical Theatre Anthology is the most comprehensive series of its kind ever to appear in print. Its unique perspective is in looking at the field of musical theatre in terms of vocal literature. One of the prime parameters in choosing the songs for this series was that they should all be, in some way, particularly vocally gratifying.

Many of the songs included here are very familiar to us, yet we seldom see them printed as they were originally written and performed. The long tradition in sheet music throughout this century has been to adapt a song in several ways to conform to a format which makes it accessible to the average pianist. This type of arrangement is what one finds in vocal selections, or in any piano/vocal collection of show music. These sheet arrangements serve their purpose very well, but aren't really the best performing editions for a singer. In contrast, the selections in this series have been excerpted from the original vocal scores. One of the many benefits of this is a much more satisfying piano accompaniment. In addition, many songs here have never been available separately from the full vocal scores.

In some cases, a song has required some adaptation in order to be excerpted from a show's vocal score. The practice of performing arias as removed from their operatic context gives many precedents for making such adjustments. In many ways, one could view this anthology as a "performing edition." Significant editorial adjustments are indicated by footnotes in some instances.

The original keys of this literature (which are used here) can give important information to a singer about the nature of a song and how it should sound, and in most cases they will work very well for most singers. But, unlike opera, these original keys do not necessarily need to be reverently maintained. With some musical theatre literature, a singer should not rule out transposing a song up or down for vocal comfort.

There is certainly no codified system for classifying theatre music as to voice type. With some roles the classification is obvious. With others there is a good deal of ambiguity. As a result, a particular singer might find suitable literature in this anthology in both volumes of his/her gender.

Any performer of these songs will benefit greatly by a careful study of the show and role from which any given song is taken. This type of approach is taken for granted with an actor preparing a monologue or an opera singer preparing an aria. But because much theatre music has been the popular music of its time, we sometimes easily lose awareness of its dramatic context.

The selections in **The Singer's Musical Theatre Anthology** will certainly be significant additions to a singer's repertory, but no anthology can include every wonderful song. There is a vast body of literature, some of it virtually unknown, waiting to be discovered and brought to life.

The substantially altered Revised Edition of Mezzo-Soprano/Belter Volume 1 answers a criticism made of the selections included in the original edition. An earnest attempt was made in the original edition to accommodate a classical mezzo-soprano range and a theatre belting range all in one collection. The Revised Edition confines the repertoire to a theatre range; some selections have, therefore, been moved to Soprano volumes. Classically defined mezzo-sopranos will still find many of the songs in this volume comfortable, but also may wish to consult the Soprano volumes for further options. Additionally, there was an attempt to add many terrific songs not previously in **The Singer's Musical Theatre Anthology**: "I Got the Sun in the Morning," "Cabaret," "Some People," "Stepsisters' Lament," "Broadway Baby" and "Diamonds Are a Girl's Best Friend" are among the great new choices in the revision.

Richard Walters, editor
December, 1986

Contents

Pianists on the Recordings:

[1] Brian Dean   [2] Sue Malmberg   [3] Ruben Piirainen   [4] Christopher Ruck   [5] Richard Walters

The price of this publication includes access to companion recorded accompaniments online,
for download or streaming, using the unique code found on the title page.
Visit **www.halleonard.com/mylibrary** and enter the access code.

ABOUT THE SHOWS

The material in this section is by Stanley Green, Richard Walters, and Robert Viagas,
some of which was previously published elsewhere.

ANNIE GET YOUR GUN

MUSIC AND LYRICS: Irving Berlin
BOOK: Herbert and Dorothy Fields
DIRECTOR: Joshua Logan
CHOREOGRAPHER: Helen Tamiris
OPENED: 5/16/46, New York; a run of 1,147 performances

Irving Berlin's musical biography of scrappy gal sharpshooter Annie Oakley earned standing ovations for Broadway stars of two generations: the original, Ethel Merman, in the 1940s; and Bernadette Peters in the 1990s. The tune-packed musical traces Annie's rise from illiterate hillbilly to international marksmanship star as she's discovered and developed in the traveling "Buffalo Bill's Wild West Show." She falls hard for the show's chauvinistic male star, Frank Butler. And romance blossoms, right up until Annie begins to outshine Frank. Annie gets two chances to express her folksy philosophies in song. She proclaims the glories of the simple life in "I Got the Sun in the Morning," and the comically bawdy pleasures of that life in "Doin' What Comes Natur'lly."

ANYONE CAN WHISTLE

MUSIC AND LYRICS: Stephen Sondheim
BOOK: Arthur Laurents
CHOREOGRAPHER: Herbert Ross
OPENED: 4/4/64, New York

Something of a "cult" musical, *Anyone Can Whistle* is an allegorical satire in which Angela Lansbury (in her first Broadway musical) played a corrupt mayor of a bankrupt town who comes up with a scheme to attract tourists: a fake miracle in which a stream of water appears to spout out of solid rock. The town soon becomes a mecca for the gullible and the pious, but the hoax is exposed when the inmates of a mental institution called the Cookie Jar get mixed up with the pilgrims. Harry Guardino played a candidate for the booby hatch, mistaken for the new doctor, and Lee Remick was the head nurse, so inhibited, she was unable to whistle.

BABES IN ARMS

MUSIC: Richard Rodgers
LYRICS: Lorenz Hart
BOOK: Richard Rodgers and Lorenz Hart
CHOREOGRAPHER: George Balanchine
DIRECTOR: Robert Sinclair
OPENED: 4/14/37; a run of 289 performances

With such songs as "I Wish I Were in Love Again," "Johnny One Note," "The Lady Is a Tramp," "My Funny Valentine," and "Where or When," *Babes in Arms* boasted more hits than any of Rodgers and Hart's twenty-nine stage musicals. In the high-spirited, youthful show, a group of youngsters, whose parents are out-of-work vaudevillians, stage a revue to keep from being sent to a work farm. Unfortunately, the show is not a success. Later, when a transatlantic French flyer lands nearby, they attract enough publicity to put on a successful show and have their own youth center. Among the cast's babes in arms were such future stars as Alfred Drake and Dan Dailey, both appearing in their first Broadway roles. MGM's 1939 film version, starring Mickey Rooney and Judy Garland, retained only two of the Rodgers and Hart songs. The director was Busby Berkeley.

CABARET

MUSIC: John Kander
LYRICS: Fred Ebb
BOOK: Joe Masteroff
DIRECTOR: Harold Prince
CHOREOGRAPHER: Ron Field
OPENED: 11/20/66, New York; a run of 1,165 performances

This moody musical captures the morally corrupt world of Berlin's demimonde just as the Nazis were coming to power. American writer Cliff Bradshaw moves in with Sally Bowles, the hedonistic star singer at a seedy nightclub. Soon, he comes to see all of Germany through the dark lens of that increasingly menacing cabaret, which is ruled over by a ghostly Emcee. Sally is introduced when she bounds onto the cabaret stage to sing the finger-wagging "Don't Tell Mama," the comic account of her scandalous fall into life as a chorus cutie. She explains her hell-bent philosophy of life in the show's title song, "Cabaret." And on a much more somber note, her landlady tries to rationalize why she broke off her engagement to a nice Jewish man in "What Would You Do?".

CALL ME MADAM

MUSIC AND LYRICS: Irving Berlin
BOOK: Howard Lindsay and Russell Crouse
DIRECTOR: George Abbott
CHOREOGRAPHER: Jerome Robbins
OPENED: 10/12/50, New York; a run of 644 performances

Annie Get Your Gun provided the biggest hit of two big careers: Irving Berlin's and Ethel Merman's. Small wonder that just four years later they were collaborating again on a musical about another vivid real-life character. This time, they developed a tale of Sally, a former Washington party-giver, who gets named ambassador to a tiny European country, "Lichtenburg." The story is based on the life of Perle Mesta, whom President Harry Truman had appointed ambassador to Luxembourg two years earlier. The show pokes fun at politics, foreign affairs, and the familiar sight of comically gauche Americans abroad. Never heard of Sally? No problem: She bounds downstage with typical Merman directness to tell the audience exactly who she is: "The Hostess with the Mostes' on the Ball." Other characters include Sally's young aide who falls in love with Lichtenburg's prince. A rarely-seen film version of the musical was released in 1953, also starring Merman.

CATS

MUSIC: Andrew Lloyd Webber
LYRICS: T.S. Eliot
DIRECTOR: Trevor Nunn
CHOREOGRAPHER: Gillian Lynne
OPENED: London, 5/11/81; a run of 8,949 performances; New York, 10/7/82; a run of 7,485 performances

Charged with energy, flair and imagination, this feline fantasy proved to be equally successful on Broadway where it was even more of an environmental experience than in the West End. With the entire Winter Garden theatre transformed into one enormous junkyard, theatregoers were confronted with such unexpected sights as outsized garbagy objects spilling into the audience, the elimination of the proscenium arch, and a ceiling that has been lowered and transformed into a twinkling canopy suggesting both cats' eyes and stars. Adapted from T.S. Eliot's collection of poems, *Old Possum's Book of Practical Cats*, the song-and-dance spectacle introduces such whimsical characters as the mysterious Mr. Mistoffelees, the patriarchal Old Deuteronomy, Skimbleshanks the Railway Cat, and Jennyanydots, the Old Gumbie Cat who sits all day and becomes active only at night. The musical's song hit, "Memory," is sung by Grizabella, the faded Glamour Cat, who, at the evening's end, ascends to the cats' heaven known as the Heaviside Layer.

CHICAGO

MUSIC: John Kander
LYRICS: Fred Ebb
BOOK: Fred Ebb and Bob Fosse
DIRECTOR-CHOREOGRAPHER: Bob Fosse
OPENED: 6/3/75, New York; a run of 872 performances

Based on Maureen Dallas Watkins' 1926 play *Roxie Hart*, this tough, flint-hearted musical tells the story of Roxie, a married chorus girl who kills her faithless lover. She manages to win release from prison through the histrionic efforts of razzle-dazzle lawyer Billy Flynn, and ends up as a vaudeville headliner with another "scintillating sinner," Velma Kelly. This scathing indictment of the American legal system, political system, media and morals may have been ahead of its time in its original 1975 production (it was also overshadowed by the opening of *A Chorus Line* the same season). But it came roaring back for a stylish, Tony-winning 1996 revival that has already run longer than the original. Roxie expresses her complete lack of conscience in song. In "Funny Honey," she sings the praises of her ever-loyal and slightly dim husband—until he starts to figure out what's going on.

A CHORUS LINE

MUSIC: Marvin Hamlisch
LYRICS: Ed Kleban
BOOK: James Kirkwood and Nicholas Dante
DIRECTOR: Michael Bennett
CHOREOGRAPHER: Michael Bennett and Bob Avian
OPENED: 7/25/75, New York; a run of 6,137 performances

Until overtaken by *Cats*, this musical stood for years as the longest-running show in Broadway history. It also won numerous Tony Awards, including Best Musical, plus the Pulitzer Prize for drama. The plot is simple: seventeen dancers reveal their life stories as they audition and compete for eight chorus parts in an unnamed Broadway musical. The show concentrates on the joys and troubles of their childhood and the teen years. One of the pretty female dancers is very proud of her body, and she should be: she designed and paid for it. Her "Dance: Ten; Looks: Three" is a joyous, extroverted paean to the benefits of plastic surgery. The song contains some PG-13 language.

CINDERELLA

MUSIC: Richard Rodgers
LYRICS AND BOOK: Oscar Hammerstein II
DIRECTOR: Ralph Nelson
CHOREOGRAPHER: Jonathan Lucas
FIRST AIRED: 3/31/57 on CBS-TV

Ever the innovators, Rodgers and Hammerstein were among the first to explore the new medium of television with a full-length original TV musical. The original broadcast also was fortunate in securing the services of Julie Andrews, fresh from her triumph as the Cinderella-like heroine of *My Fair Lady*. In adapting the children's fairy tale, Hammerstein was careful not to alter or update the familiar story about a young woman who collaborates with her Fairy Godmother to overcome the plots of her evil stepmother and stepsisters so she can go to an opulent ball and meet a handsome prince. Cinderella still loses her magical glass slipper, and the Prince still proclaims that he will marry the girl whose foot fits the slipper. Because the original production was filmed live and could not be preserved except in black-and-white kinescope, a new production was captured on tape in 1965. Starring Lesley Ann Warren, this second version is the one that's been aired numerous times and even released on video. A stage adaptation toured the U.S., and the musical finally made its New York stage debut in 1993 at New York City Opera, with Christa Moore as Cinderella. At the ball, the prince is stunned by how quickly he's fallen in love with this ravishing stranger. Jealously watching him from the sidelines, the unpalatable sing the comic "Stepsisters' Lament," in which they gripe about the unfair way pleasant, attractive women have of getting all the best guys.

EVITA

MUSIC: Andrew Lloyd Webber
LYRICS AND BOOK: Tim Rice
DIRECTOR: Harold Prince
CHOREOGRAPHER: Larry Fuller
OPENED: London, 6/23/78; a run of 2,900 performances; New York, 9/25/79; a run of 1,567 performances

Because of its great success in London, *Evita* was practically a pre-sold hit when it began its run on Broadway. Based on events in the life of Argentina's strong-willed leader, Eva Peron, the musical—with Patti LuPone in the title role—traced her rise from struggling actress to wife of dictator Juan Peron (Bob Gunton), and virtual co-ruler of the country. Though the plot was told entirely through song and had originally been conceived as a project for records, the razzle-dazzle staging of Harold Prince turned *Evita* into an exciting theatrical concept that has been hailed throughout the world. Of no little help, of course, has been the universal popularity of the haunting melody, "Don't Cry for Me Argentina."

FINIAN'S RAINBOW

MUSIC: Burton Lane
LYRICS: E.Y. Harburg
BOOK: E.Y. Harburg and Fred Saidy
DIRECTOR: Bretaigne Windust
CHOREOGRAPHER: Michael Kidd
OPENED: 1/10/47, New York; a run of 725 performances

Finian's Rainbow evolved out of co-librettist E.Y. Harburg's desire to satirize an economic system that requires gold reserves to be buried in the ground at Fort Knox. This led to the idea of leprechauns and the crock of gold that, according to legend, could grant three wishes. The story takes place in Rainbow Valley, Missitucky, and involves Finian McLonergan, an Irish immigrant, and his efforts to bury a crock of gold which, he is sure, will grow and make him rich. Also involved are Og, a leprechaun from whom the crock has been stolen, Finian's daughter, Sharon, who dreams wistfully of Glocca Morra, and Woody Mahony, a labor organizer who blames that "Old Devil Moon" for the way he feels about Sharon. In the 1968 Warner Bros. adaptation, Fred Astaire played Finian, Petula Clark was his daughter, and Tommy Steele was the leprechaun. The director was Francis Coppola.

FLOWER DRUM SONG

MUSIC: Richard Rodgers
LYRICS: Oscar Hammerstein II
BOOK: Oscar Hammerstein II and Joseph Fields
DIRECTOR: Gene Kelly
CHOREOGRAPHER: Carol Haney
OPENED: 12/1/58, New York; a run of 600 performances

It was librettist Joseph Fields who first secured the rights to C.Y. Lee's novel and then approached Rodgers and Hammerstein to join him as collaborators. To dramatize the conflict between traditionalist older Chinese-Americans living in San Francisco and their thoroughly Americanized offspring, the musical tells the story of Mei Li, a timid "picture bride" from China, who arrives to fulfill her contract to marry nightclub owner Sammy Fong. Sammy, however, prefers dancer Linda Low. The problem is resolved when Sammy's friend Wang Ta discovers that Mei Li really is the bride for him. Linda sings a bouncy tribute to the life of lipstick, lace and flowers in "I Enjoy Being a Girl."

FOLLIES

MUSIC AND LYRICS: Stephen Sondheim
BOOK: James Goldman
DIRECTOR: Harold Prince
CHOREOGRAPHER: Michael Bennett
OPENED: 4/4/71, New York; a run of 522 performances

Taking place at a reunion of former Ziegfeld Follies-type showgirls, the musical deals with the reality of life as contrasted with the unreality of the theatre. *Follies* explores this theme through the lives of two couples, the upper-class, unhappy, Phyllis and Benjamin Stone, and the middle-class, also unhappy, Sally and Buddy Plummer. *Follies* also shows us these four as they were in their pre-marital youth. The young actors appear as ghosts to haunt their elder selves. Because the show is about the past, and often in flashback, Sondheim styled his songs to evoke some of the theatre's great composers and lyricists of the past, with a cast that suggests some of the vivid personalities of 1920s Broadway. In the showstopping anthem "Broadway Baby," veteran actress Hattie Walker evokes the innocence and gutsy determination of herself when she was just starting out.

GENTLEMEN PREFER BLONDES

MUSIC: Jule Styne
LYRICS: Leo Robin
BOOK: Joseph Stein and Anita Loos
DIRECTOR: John C. Wilson
CHOREOGRAPHER: Agnes de Mille
OPENED: 12/8/49, New York; a run of 740 performances

Based on Anita Loos' popular 1926 novel and play of the same name, *Gentlemen Prefer Blondes* took a satirical look at the wacky, gold-digging world of 1920s flappers. Playing Lorelei Lee, the husband-hunting "Little Girl from Little Rock," Carol Channing scored a star-making success in her first major role. The show's action takes place mostly aboard the liner *Ile de France*, which is taking Lorelei and her chum Dorothy Paris, courtesy of Lorelei's generous friend, button tycoon Gus Esmond. En route, the girls meet a number of accommodating gentlemen, and romantic complications ensue. Lorelei rolls out her philosophy of life in the march "Diamonds Are a Girl's Best Friend." A 1953 film version (minus much of the score) starred Marilyn Monroe and Jane Russell. The song "Ain't There Anyone Here for Love?" was written for the film version, a memorable number with Jane Russell in a gym full of men totally ignoring her. A new Broadway version in 1973 extensively changed the score, and was retitled *Lorelei*.

GODSPELL

MUSIC AND LYRICS: Stephen Schwartz
BOOK AND DIRECTION: John-Michael Tebelak
OPENED: 5/17/71, New York; a run of 2,124 Off-Broadway, then 527 on Broadway

With its rock-flavored score, *Godspell* is a contemporary, flower-child view of the Gospel of St. Matthew. Christ, depicted as a clown-faced innocent with a Superman "S" on his shirt, leads a band of followers in dramatized parables, including the Prodigal Son, the Good Samaritan, the Pharisee and the Tax Collector. Originating as a nonmusical play at the experimental Café La Mama, the show added words and music by Stephen Schwartz and began its Off-Broadway run at the Cherry Lane Theatre in Greenwich Village. It soon transferred to the Promenade, where it remained for more than five years. Beginning in June 1976, it also had a Broadway run. The show was a hit in London as well, and was filmed by Columbia. The funky "Turn Back, O Man" was sung by the troupe's scarlet woman, who bumped her way up and down the aisles of the theatre during her rendition.

GUYS AND DOLLS

MUSIC AND LYRICS: Frank Loesser
BOOK: Abe Burrows and Jo Swerling
DIRECTOR: George S. Kaufman
CHOREOGRAPHER: Michael Kidd
OPENED: 11/24/50, New York; a run of 1,200 performances

Populated by the hard-shelled but soft-centered characters who inhabit the world of writer Damon Runyon, this "Musical Fable of Broadway" tells the tale of how Miss Sarah Brown of the Save-A-Soul Mission saves the souls of assorted Times Square riff-raff while losing her heart to the smooth-talking gambler, Sky Masterson. A more comic romance involves Nathan Detroit, who runs the "oldest established permanent floating crap game in New York," and Miss Adelaide, the star of the Hot Box nightclub to whom he has been engaged for fourteen years. As part of her club act, Miss Adelaide sings "Take Back Your Mink," expressing mock outrage to an unseen swain who has presumed to think she's "that kind of a girl." As she pulls off his gifts of clothing and fur and throws them back in his face, she's actually doing an elegant striptease.

GYPSY

MUSIC: Jule Styne
LYRICS: Stephen Sondheim
BOOK: Arthur Laurents
DIRECTOR AND CHOREOGRAPHER: Jerome Robbins
OPENED: 5/21/59, New York; a run of 702 performances

Written for Ethel Merman, who gave the performance of her career as Gypsy Rose Lee's ruthless, domineering mother, *Gypsy* is one of the great scores in the mature musical comedy tradition. The idea for the musical began with producer David Merrick, who needed to read only one chapter in Miss Lee's autobiography to convince him of its stage potential. Originally, Stephen Sondheim was to have supplied the music as well as the lyrics, but Miss Merman, who had just come from a lukewarm production on Broadway, wanted the more experienced Jule Styne. In the story, Mama Rose is determined to escape from her humdrum life by pushing the vaudeville career of her daughter, June. After June runs away to get married, Mama focuses all her attention on her other daughter, the previously neglected Louise. As vaudeville declines, so do their fortunes, until an accidental booking at a burlesque theatre and Louise's ad-libbed striptease turn Louise into a star—the legendary Gypsy Rose Lee. Rose achieves a version of her dream, but suffers a breakdown when she realizes that she is no longer needed in her daughter's career. Several major stars have played Mama Rose. Rosalind Russell won the role in the 1962 film. Angela Lansbury toplined a successful mid-1970s revival in London and in New York. Tyne Daly gave the role a new spin in 1989. Bette Midler brought the show to a wider audience in a mid-1990s TV adaptation. Coming near the top of the show, "Some People" is Rose's indictment of all that is dull, boring and ordinary in life, and expresses her resolution to grab for more.

HOW TO SUCCEED IN BUSINESS WITHOUT REALLY TRYING

MUSIC AND LYRICS: Frank Loesser
BOOK: Abe Burrows, based on a play by Jack Weinstock and Willie Gilbert
DIRECTOR: Abe Burrows
CHOREOGRAPHER: Bob Fosse and Hugh Lambert
OPENED: 10/14/61, New York; a run of 1,417 performances

Based on the book by Shepherd Mead, *Business* traces the career of J. Pierpont Finch as he climbs from the mailroom to CEO in a few easy steps—not by hard work, but by explicitly following the advice of a book called "How to Succeed in Business Without Really Trying." Finch is a boyish, charming, but ruthless character, a satirical twist on the Horatio Alger-ish American myth. The show takes swipes at such business mainstays as Yes Men, coffee breaks, nepotism, office parties, and boardroom presentations. Looking for a bright young exec on his way up, Rosemary sets her cap for Finch, outlining her vision for contented housewifehood in "Happy to Keep His Dinner Warm." The show won the Pulitzer Prize for drama, only the fourth musical to do so. A movie version, virtually a filming of the staged production, was released in 1967, again with Robert Morse in the role of Finch.

KISS ME, KATE

MUSIC AND LYRICS: Cole Porter
BOOK: Samuel and Bella Spewack
DIRECTOR: John C. Wilson
CHOREOGRAPHER: Hanya Holm
OPENED: 12/30/48, New York; a run of 1,077 performances

The genesis of Cole Porter's longest-running musical occurred in 1935 when producer Saint Subber, then a stagehand for the Theatre Guild's production of Shakespeare's *Taming of the Shrew*, became aware that its stars Alfred Lunt and Lynn Fontanne, quarreled almost as much in private as did the characters in the play. Years later he offered this parallel story as the basis for a musical comedy to the same writing trio, Porter and the Spewacks, who had already worked on the successful show, *Leave It to Me!* The entire action of *Kiss Me, Kate* occurs backstage and onstage at Ford's Theatre, Baltimore during a tryout of a musical version of *The Taming of the Shrew*. The main plot concerns the egotistical actor-producer Fred Graham (Alfred Drake) and his temperamental ex-wife Lili Vanessi (Patricia Morison) who—like Shakespeare's Petruchio and Kate—fight and make up and eventually demonstrate their enduring affection for each other. One of the chief features of the score is the skillful way Cole Porter combined his own musical world ("So in Love," "Too Darn Hot," and "Why Can't You Behave?") with Shakespeare's world ("I Hate Men"), while also tossing off a Viennese waltz parody ("Wunderbar") and a comic view of the Bard's plays ("Brush Up Your Shakespeare").

A LITTLE NIGHT MUSIC

MUSIC AND LYRICS: Stephen Sondheim
BOOK: Hugh Wheeler
DIRECTOR: Harold Prince
CHOREOGRAPHER: Patricia Birch
OPENED: 2/25/73, New York; a run of 601 performances

Based on Ingmar Bergman's 1955 film, *Smiles of a Summer Night, A Little Night Music* could claim two musical distinctions: the entire Stephen Sondheim score was composed in 3/4 time (or multiples thereof) and it contained, in "Send in the Clowns," the biggest song hit that Sondheim ever wrote. The musical took a somewhat jaded look at a group of well-to-do Swedes at the turn of the century, among them a lawyer, Fredrick Egerman, his virginal child bride, Anne, his former mistress, the actress Desirée Armfeldt, Desirée's current lover, the aristocratic Count Carl-Magnus Malcolm, and the count's suicidal wife, Charlotte. Eventually, the proper partners are sorted out during a weekend at the country house of Desirée's mother, a former concubine of European nobility. A film version was released by New World Pictures in 1978, with Elizabeth Taylor (Desirée), Len Cariou, Diana Rigg (Charlotte), and Hermione Gingold. The director was Harold Prince and the locale switched to Vienna.

OKLAHOMA!

MUSIC: Richard Rodgers
LYRICS AND BOOK: Oscar Hammerstein II
DIRECTOR: Rouben Mamoulian
CHOREOGRAPHER: Agnes de Mille
OPENED: 3/31/43, New York; a run of 2,212 performances

There are many reasons why *Oklahoma!* is a recognized landmark in the history of American musical theatre. In the initial collaboration between Richard Rodgers and Oscar Hammerstein II, it not only expertly fused the major elements in the production—story, songs and dances—it also utilized dream ballets to reveal hidden desires and fears of the principals. In addition, the musical, based on Lynn Riggs' play, *Green Grow the Lilacs*, was the first with a book that honestly depicted the kind of rugged pioneers who had once tilled the land and tended the cattle. Set in Indian Territory soon after the turn of the century, *Oklahoma!* spins a simple tale mostly concerned with whether the decent Curly (Alfred Drake) or the menacing Jud (Howard Da Silva) gets to take Laurey (Joan Roberts) to the box social. Though she chooses Jud in a fit of pique, Laurey really loves Curly and they soon make plans to marry. At their wedding they join in celebrating Oklahoma's impending statehood, then—after Jud is accidentally killed in a fight with Curly—the couple rides off in their surrey with the fringe on top. With its Broadway run of five years, nine months, *Oklahoma!* established a long-run record that it held for fifteen years. It also toured the United States and Canada for over a decade. In 1979, the musical was revived on Broadway with a cast headed by Laurence Guittard and Christine Andreas, and ran for 293 performances. The film version, the first in Todd-AO, was released by Magna in 1955. Gordon MacRae, Shirley Jones and Charlotte Greenwood were in it, and the director was Fred Zinnemann.

ON A CLEAR DAY YOU CAN SEE FOREVER

MUSIC: Burton Lane
LYRICS AND BOOK: Alan Jay Lerner
BOOK: Alfred Uhry
DIRECTOR: Robert Lewis
CHOREOGRAPHER: Herbert Ross
OPENED: 10/17/65, New York; a run of 280 performances

Alan Jay Lerner's fascination with the phenomenon of extrasensory perception led to his teaming with composer Richard Rodgers in 1962 to write a musical to be called *I Picked a Daisy*. When that didn't work out, Lerner turned to composer Burton Lane, with whom he'd worked in Hollywood years before. The result is a show about Daisy Gamble, who not only predicts the future, but under hypnosis by Dr. Mark Bruckner, can recall her past life as Melinda Wells in 18th century London. Mark discovers her powers of ESP and quickly assures her she isn't abnormal, simply "ahead" in that department. Mark becomes infatuated with Melinda, who becomes a romantic rival to the present-day Daisy. They split up, but he persuades her to "Come Back to Me" in the up-tempo entreaty of the same title. Barbra Streisand starred in the 1970 Vincente Minnelli filmed version of the musical.

SOUTH PACIFIC

MUSIC: Richard Rodgers
LYRICS: Oscar Hammerstein II
BOOK: Oscar Hammerstein II and Joshua Logan
DIRECTOR: Joshua Logan
OPENED: 4/7/49, New York; a run of 1,925 performances

South Pacific had the second longest Broadway run of the nine musicals with songs by Richard Rodgers and Oscar Hammerstein II. Director Joshua Logan first urged the partners to adapt a short story, "Fo' Dolla," contained in James Michener's book about World War II, *Tales of the South Pacific*. Rodgers and Hammerstein, however, felt that the story—about Lt. Joe Cable's tender romance with Liat, a Polynesian girl—was a bit too much like *Madame Butterfly*, and they suggested that another story in the collection, "Our Heroine," should provide the main plot. This one was about the unlikely attraction between Nellie Forbush, a naive Navy nurse from Little Rock, and Emile de Becque, a sophisticated French planter living on a Pacific island. The tales were combined by having Cable and de Becque go on a dangerous mission together behind Japanese lines. Coming just a few years after the war, and featuring several veterans in the cast, the show was enormously resonant with 1949 audiences. Perhaps because of its daring (for the time) theme of the evils of racial prejudice, it was also the second musical to be awarded the prestigious Pulitzer Prize for Drama. This production was the first of two musicals (the other was *The Sound of Music*) in which Mary Martin, who played Nellie, was seen as a Rodgers and Hammerstein heroine. It also marked the Broadway debut of famed Metropolitan Opera basso, Ezio Pinza, who played de Becque. Mitzi Gaynor and Rossano Brazzi starred in 20th Century-Fox's 1958 film version, also directed by Logan.

SWEENEY TODD, THE DEMON BARBER OF FLEET STREET

MUSIC AND LYRICS: Stephen Sondheim
BOOK: Hugh Wheeler
DIRECTOR: Harold Prince
OPENED: 3/1/79, New York; a run of 557 performances

Despite the sordidness of its main plot—a half mad, vengeance-obsessed barber in Victorian London slits the throats of his customers whose corpses are then turned into meat pies by his accomplice, Mrs. Lovett—this near-operatic musical is a bold and often brilliant depiction of the cannibalizing effects of the Industrial Revolution. Sweeney Todd first appeared on the London stage in 1842 in a play called *A String of Pearls*, or *The Fiend of Fleet Street*. Other versions followed, the most recent being Christopher Bond's *Sweeney Todd*, produced in 1973, which served as the basis of the musical. Sondheim's masterwork is quickly gaining a foothold in the operatic repertory, with prominent productions at Houston and the New York City Opera.

TWO BY TWO

MUSIC: Richard Rodgers
LYRICS: Martin Charnin
BOOK: Peter Stone
DIRECTOR: Joe Layton
OPENED: 1/10/70, New York

After an absence of almost thirty years, Danny Kaye returned to Broadway in a musical based on the legend of Noah and the Ark. Adapted from Clifford Odets' play, *The Flowering Peach*, *Two by Two* dealt primarily with Noah's rejuvenation and his relationship with his wife and family as he undertakes the formidable task that God has commanded. During the run, Kaye suffered a torn ligament in his left leg and was briefly hospitalized. He returned hobbling on a crutch with his leg in a cast, a situation he used as an excuse to depart from the script by cutting up and clowning around. For his third musical following Oscar Hammerstein's death, composer Richard Rodgers joined lyricist Martin Charnin (later to be responsible for *Annie*) to create a melodious score that included "An Old Man."

THE UNSINKABLE MOLLY BROWN

MUSIC AND LYRICS: Meredith Willson
BOOK: Richard Morris
DIRECTOR: Dore Schary
CHOREOGRAPHER: Peter Gennaro
OPENED: 11/3/60, New York; a run of 532 performances

Having made his Broadway bow with *The Music Man*, composer Meredith Willson had a tough act to follow. He chose another rural American subject, real-life feisty Colorado mining millionairess Molly Brown, whose life is also changed in 1912. Determined to leave the poverty of her girlhood far behind, she meets and marries rough-hewn mining wunderkind Leadville Johnny Brown, rises to the top of Denver society, then sets out to conquer Europe. Her odyssey lands her on the Titanic, where once again her determination literally to rise above it all stands her in very good stead, and earns her the nickname of the title. Having created, in "Seventy Six Trombones," the most memorable American march since the age of John Phillip Sousa, Willson tried again, coming up with the infectious "I Ain't Down Yet," which bursts with Molly's unique brand of spunk.

I GOT THE SUN IN THE MORNING

from the stage production *Annie Get Your Gun*

Words and Music by
IRVING BERLIN

Allegro moderato

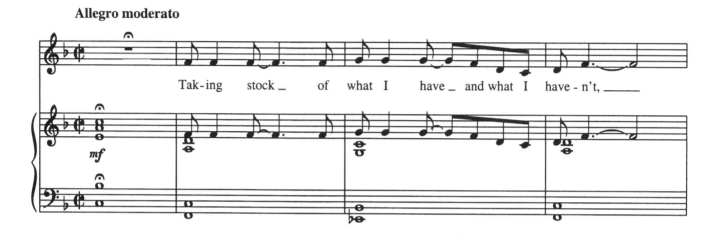

Tak-ing stock _ of what I have _ and what I have-n't, _____

What do I find? _ The things I have will keep me sat-is-fied. _____

_ Check-ing up _ on what I have _ and what I have-n't _____

What do I find? __ A health-y bal-ance on the cred-it side. __

Bounce (♫ = ♩♪)

Got no dia-mond, got no pearl, __ Still I think __ I'm a
Got no but-ler, got no maid, __ Still I think __ I've been

luck-y girl, __ I got the sun in the morn-ing and the moon at night. __
o-ver paid, __ I got the sun in the morn-ing and the moon at night. __

Got no man-sion, got no yacht, __
Got no sil-ver, got no gold, __

DOIN' WHAT COMES NATUR'LLY

from the stage production *Annie Get Your Gun*

Words and Music by
IRVING BERLIN

Folks are dumb where I come from They ain't had an-y learn-in',
Un-cle Jed has nev-er read An al-man-ac on drink-in'

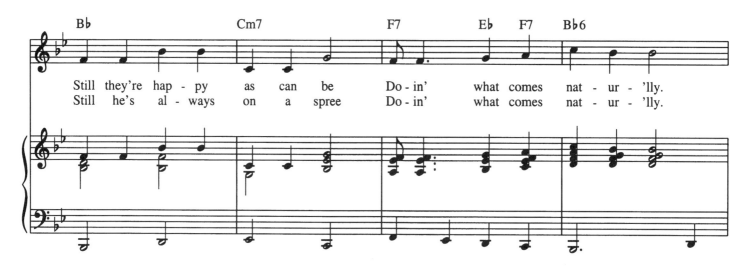

Still they're hap-py as can be Do-in' what comes nat-ur-'lly.
Still he's al-ways on a spree Do-in' what comes nat-ur-'lly.

Folks like us could nev-er fuss With
Sis-ter Sal who's mu-si-cal Has

19

know they had no learn - in'
some - one he just mar - ried.

Still they raised a fam - i - ly
There he is at nine - ty - three

Do - in' what comes nat - ur - 'lly.
Do - in' what comes nat - ur - 'lly.

ANYONE CAN WHISTLE

from *Anyone Can Whistle*

Words and Music by
STEPHEN SONDHEIM

May-be you could show me how to let go, low-er my guard,

learn to be free, May-be if you whis -tle, whis - tle for me.

I can slay a dra-gon an-y old week -- Eas-y. _____ What's

hard is sim - ple. What's nat-u-ral comes hard.

May-be you could show me how to let go, low-er my guard, learn to be free.

May-be if you whis-tle, whis-tle for me. _____

THE LADY IS A TRAMP

from *Babes in Arms*

Words by LORENZ HART
Music by RICHARD RODGERS

Ca-'ad. But so-cial cir-cles spin too fast for me. My

[In tempo]

ho - bo - hem - ia is the place to be.

I get too hun-gry for din - ner at eight.
I go to Con - ey, The beach is di - vine.

I like the thea-tre, but nev - er come late.
I go to ball games, the bleach-ers are fine.

Won't dish the dirt with the rest of the girls,—
I go to op-era and stay wide a-wake,—

That's why the la-dy is a tramp! _____ I like the
That's why the la-dy is a tramp! _____ I like the

free fresh wind in my hair,—
green grass un-der my shoes.—

Life with-out care.— I'm broke,— It's oke!—
What can I lose?— I'm flat!— That's that!—

mf

Hate Cal - i - forn - ia, it's cold and it's damp,___
I'm all a - lone when I low - er my lamp,___

1.
That's why the la - dy is a tramp!___

2.
That's why the la - dy is a

tramp.___

DON'T TELL MAMA
from the musical *Cabaret*

Words by FRED EBB
Music by JOHN KANDER

Sally sings this number with the chorus.

Ma - ma does-n't e - ven have an

ink - ling That I'm work-ing in a night - club

In a pair of lac - y pants. So

Slowly, in 4

please, sir, if you run in - to my ma - ma, Don't re-veal my in - dis-

I would nev-er tell __ on you. _____ I'm

break-ing ev-'ry prom-ise that I gave __ her, _____ So

won't you kind-ly do a girl a great big fav - or? __ And

please, my __ sweet pa - ta - ter, Keep this __ from the ma - ter,

Though my dance is not a-gainst the law. _____ You can

tell my Pa-pa, that's all right, _ 'Cause he comes in here

ev-'ry night, _ But don't tell Ma-ma what you

saw! _____

Ma - ma thinks I'm on a tour of Eu - rope, With a cou-ple of my

school chums And a la - dy chap-er - one. _____

Ma - ma does-n't e - ven have an ink - ling That I left them all in

Ant - werp And I'm tour-ing on my own. _____ So

If you ___ had a se-cret, You bet ___ I could keep it.

I would nev-er tell ___ on you. _____ You

would-n't want to get me in a pick - le ___

And have her go and cut me off with - out a

nick - el. __ So let's trust __ one an - oth - er, Keep this __ from my moth-er, Though I'm still as pure as moun-tain snow. __

__ You can tell my un-cle, here and now, __ 'Cause he's my a - gent an - y - how, __ But don't tell Ma-ma what you know.

Don't tell Ma-ma, please, sir. Don't tell Ma-ma what you

know. Sssh! Sssh! If you

see my mum-my, mum's the word!

WHAT WOULD YOU DO?

from the musical *Cabaret*

Words by FRED EBB
Music by JOHN KANDER

Spoken before introduction: It's easy for you to say "fight"! (intro starts)

sum of a life-time, e - ven so, I'll take your ad - vice. ____

____ What would you do? _____ Would you pay the price? ____

R.H.

____ What would you do? Sup - pose sim-ply keep-ing still ____

____ Means you man - age un - til the end?

poco rall.   *a tempo*

pose you're one fright-ened voice Be - ing told what the choice must

be, Go on, tell me, I will

lis - ten. What would you do if

you were me? _____

CABARET

from the musical *Cabaret*

Words by FRED EBB
Music by JOHN KANDER

What good is sit-ting a-lone in your room?— Come hear the mu-sic play.

Life is a cab-a-ret, old chum,—

THE HOSTESS WITH
THE MOSTES' ON THE BALL

from the stage production *Call Me Madam*

Words and Music by
IRVING BERLIN

soil. He dug and he dug and what do you think? Oil, oil,

slight rit.

oil. The mon-ey rolled in and I rolled out with a for-tune piled so high.

Wash - ing - ton was my des - ti - na - tion And now who am

Medium Bounce tempo

I? I'm the cho - sen par - ty giv - er for the

White House cli - en - tele ___ And they know that I de - liv - er What it

takes to make 'em jell. ___ And in Wash - ing - ton I'm known ___ by one and all ___

___ As the host - ess with the mos - tes' on the ball. ___

___ They would go to El - sa Max - well, When they

had an axe to grind, __ They could al - ways grind their axe __ well At the

par - ties she de - signed. __ Now the hat - chet grind - ers all __ pre - fer to call __

On the host - ess with the mos - tes' on the ball. __

I've a great big bar __ and good cav - i - ar, __ yes, the

And the host-ess with the mos-tes' on the ball.

An Am-bas-sa-dor __ has just reached the shore, __ He's a

man of man - y loves, __ An im-por-tant gent __ from the Or - i - ent __ To be

han - dled with kid gloves. __ He can come and let his hair __ down, Have the

best time of his life, ___ E - ven bring his new af - fair __ down, In - tro -

duce her as his wife. __ But she must - n't leave her pan - ties in the

hall _____ For the host - ess who's the host - ess, with the mos - tes'

on the ball. _____

MEMORY
from *Cats*

Music by ANDREW LLOYD WEBBER
Text by TREVOR NUNN after T.S. ELIOT

Freely [♩. = 50]

mp

GRIZABELLA

Mid - night._____ Not a sound from the pave - ment._____ Has the moon lost her
Me - mory_____ All a - lone in the moon - light_____ I can smile at the

me - mory?_____ She is smil-ing a - lone._____ In the
old days,_____ I was beau-ti-ful then._____ I re -

lamp - light the wi-thered leaves col - lect at my feet_____ And the
mem - ber the time I knew what hap-pi-ness was,_____ Let the

a tempo

Day - light.___ I must wait for the sun - rise,___ I must think of a new life___ And I must-n't give in.___ When the dawn comes to-night will be a me-mo-ry too___ And a new day___ will be - gin.

Burnt out ends of smo - ky days, ____ the

stale cold smell ___ of mor - ning. ____ The street lamp dies, an - o -ther

poco rit.

night is ov - er, ___ an - o -ther day is dawn - ing.

poco rit.

FUNNY HONEY

from *Chicago*

Words by FRED EBB
Music by JOHN KANDER

Tempo di Blues

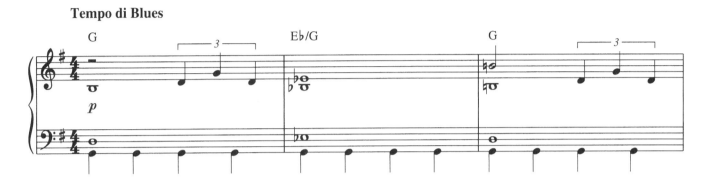

Some-times I'm right. Some-times I'm wrong. But

he does-n't care. _ He'll string a - long. _ He loves me so,

Vocal line is sung an octave lower than written.

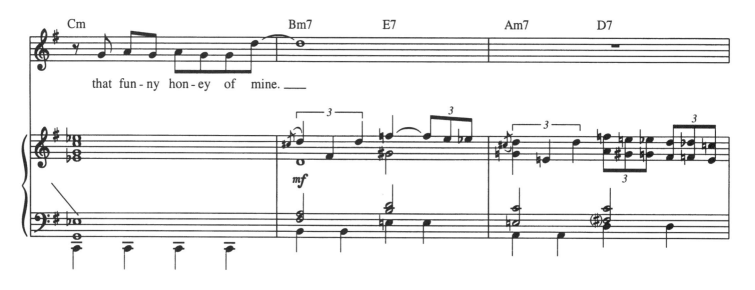

that fun - ny hon - ey of mine. ___

Some-times I'm down ____ and some-times I'm up, But he fol - lows 'round like some

droop-y-eyed pup. He loves me so, ____ that fun - ny hon - ey of mine. ___

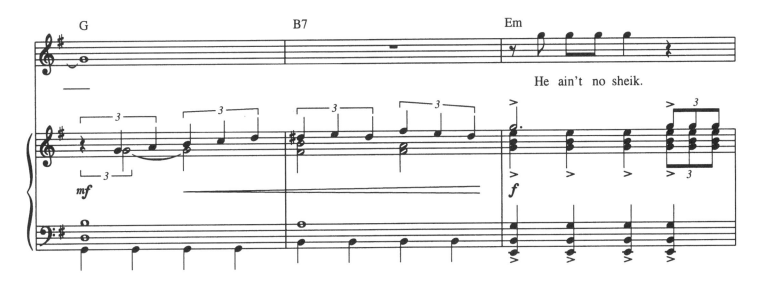

He ain't no sheik.

That's no great phy-sique. And Lord knows he ain't got the smarts. But

look at that soul! I tell ya that whole is a whole lot great-er than the

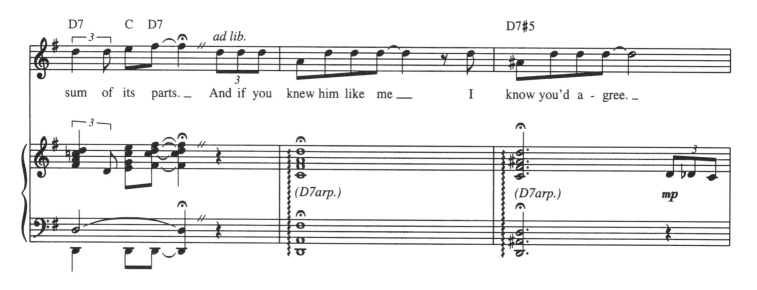

sum of its parts. __ And if you knew him like me __ I know you'd a - gree. __

What if the world slan-dered my name? __ Why he'd be right there __

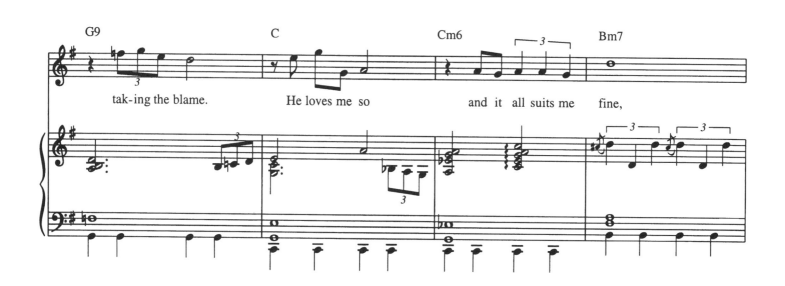

tak-ing the blame. He loves me so and it all suits me fine,

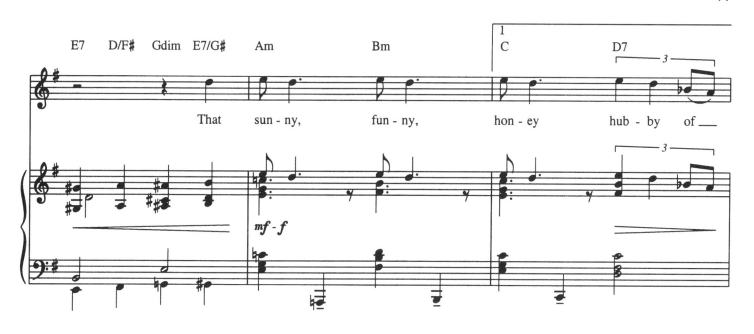

That sun - ny, fun - ny, hon - ey hub - by of ___

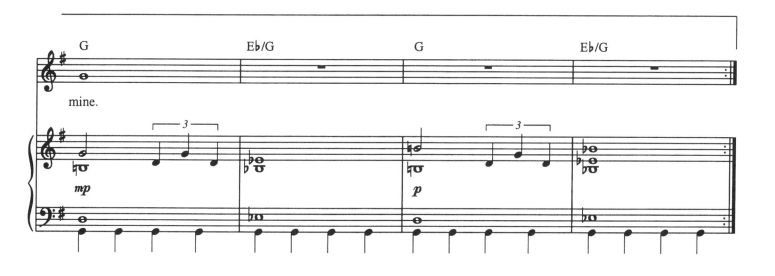

mine.

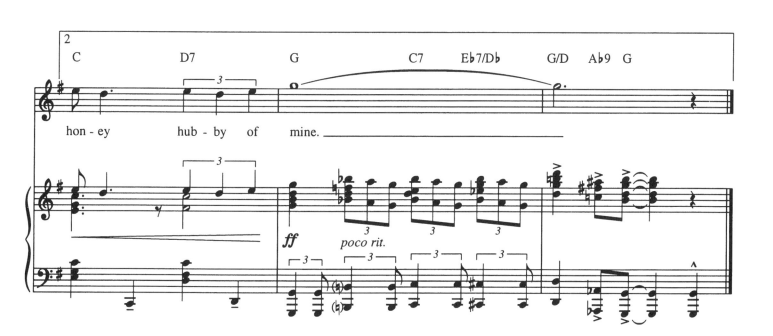

hon - ey hub - by of mine. ___

DANCE: TEN; LOOKS: THREE

from *A Chorus Line*

Music by MARVIN HAMLISCH
Lyric by EDWARD KLEBAN

HOW ARE THINGS IN GLOCCA MORRA?

from *Finian's Rainbow*

Words by E.Y. HARBURG
Music by BURTON LANE

LOOK TO THE RAINBOW

from *Finian's Rainbow*

Words by E.Y. HARBURG
Music by BURTON LANE

heart,— To sing it when - ev - er the world falls a - part.

In 3

Look, look, look to the rain - bow. Fol - low it

o - ver the hill— and stream. Look, look,

look to the rain - bow. Fol - low the fel - low who fol - lows a

dream. So I bun - dled me heart and I roamed the world free, To the

east with the lark, to the west with the sea; And I search'd all the

earth,__ and I scann'd all the skies.__ But I found it at last in my

own true love's eyes. Look, look, look to the

STEPSISTERS' LAMENT

from *Cinderella*

Lyrics by OSCAR HAMMERSTEIN II
Music by RICHARD RODGERS

March

Why would a fel-low want a girl like her, a frail and fluf - fy beau - ty?

Why can't a fel-low ev - er once pre-fer a sol - id girl like me? She's a froth-y lit - tle

Note: In the show this is sung by both sisters.

bub - ble _____ with a flim-sy kind of charm, _____ And with ver - y lit - tle

trou - ble _____ I could break her lit - tle arm! Oh, oh,

why would a fel-low want a girl like her, So ob - vious - ly un - u - sual?

Why can't a fel-low ev - er once pre - fer a u - sual girl like me? Her

why would a fel-low want a girl like her, a girl who's mere-ly

love - ly? Why can't a fel-low ev-er once pre-fer a

girl who's mere-ly me? What's the mat-ter with the man? What's the mat-ter with the

man? What's the mat-ter with the man?

DON'T CRY FOR ME ARGENTINA

from *Evita*

Lyric by TIM RICE
Music by ANDREW LLOYD WEBBER

MCA MUSIC PUBLISHING

try to ex-plain how I feel, That I still need your love af-ter all that I've done:____

____ You won't be-lieve me All you will see is a girl you once knew Al-

though she's dressed up to the nines at six-es and se-vens with you.

VERSE

2. I had to let it hap-pen, I had to change; Could-n't stay all my life down at heel: Look-ing

Horns

poco rall. . . . Slower
Refrain

love you and hope you love me. Don't cry for me Ar-gen-ti-na

(bouche fermé)
Mm m m

p colla voce

m m

dim.

Tempo I°
Refrain

Don't cry for me Ar-gen-ti-na_____ the truth is I nev-er

pp *ppp* *f*

left you: All through my wild days, my mad ex-ist-ence, I kept my prom-ise, Don't keep your

I ENJOY BEING A GIRL

from *Flower Drum Song*

Lyrics by OSCAR HAMMERSTEIN II
Music by RICHARD RODGERS

eye - lash - es all in curl, _____ I
float as the clouds on air do, _____ I en-
joy be - ing a girl. _____ When
men say I'm cute and fun - ny _____ And my

me. _____ When men say I'm sweet as can - dy, _____ As a - round in a dance we whirl, _____ It goes to my head like bran - dy, _____ I en -

When I hear the com-pli-men-t'ry whis - tle _____ That greets my bi - ki - ni by the sea, _____ I turn and I glow-er and I bris - tle, _____ But I'm hap-py to know the whis-tle's meant for me! _____ I'm strict - ly a fe - male fe - male _____

BROADWAY BABY

from *Follies*

Words and Music by
STEPHEN SONDHEIM

Broad-way Ba - by, _____ Learn-ing how to sing and dance, _

Wait-ing for that one big chance _ to be in a show. _____

Gee, I'd like to be _____ on some mar - quee, _____ All twin - kling_ lights, _ a

spark to pierce the dark _____ From Bat-t'ry Park _____ to Wash - ing-ton Heights. _

Some day, may-be, _____ All my dreams will be re - paid. _____

_____ Hell, I'd e - ven play the maid _____ to be in a

show! _____ Say, Mis - ter Pro - duc - er, _____

I'm talk - ing to you, _____ sir. _____ I don't need a lot,

On - ly what I got, Plus a tube of grease-paint and a fol - low spot! _ I'm a

Broad - way Ba - by, _____ Slav - ing at a five and ten, _

_____ Dream - ing of the great day when _ I'll be in a

no swing beat

show! _____

8va - *loco*

118

COULD I LEAVE YOU

from *Follies*

Words and Music by
STEPHEN SONDHEIM

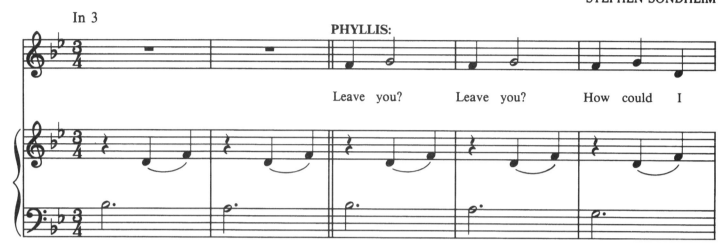

wait! I'm just be - gin - ning! What, leave you? Leave you?

How could I leave you? What would I do on my own?

R.H.

put - ting thoughts of you a - side In the south of France, Would I think of

su - i - cide? Dar - ling, shall we dance?

Could I live through the pain On a ter-race in Spain? Would it pass? It would pass. Could I bur-y my rage with a boy half your age in the grass? Bet your ass. But I've done that al-read-y,

Or did-n't you know, love? _____

Tell me, how could I leave when I left long a-

go, _____ love? _____

_R.H._

Could I leave you? No, the point is, Could you leave

nine - ty per - cent of the mon - ey you make, And the rugs And the cooks Dar - ling you keep the drugs, An - gel, you keep the books, Hon - ey,

I'll take the grand, Su - gar, you keep the

spin - et And all of our friends and.. Just

wait a god - damn min - ute! Oh, leave you? Leave you? How could I

leave you? Sweet - heart, I have to con - fess: _____

cresc. poco a poco

R.H.

LOSING MY MIND

from *Follies*

Words and Music by
STEPHEN SONDHEIM

you, Spend sleep - less nights To think __ a - bout you. You said __ you loved

me, Or were you just be - ing kind? __ *rall.* Or am I los - ing my

mind?

I want __ you so, It's like I'm los - ing my mind. __

Accelerando

Does no one know? It's like I'm los-ing my mind.

Faster *(colla voce)*

All af-ter-noon, do-ing ev-'ry lit-tle chore, The thought of you stays

bright. Some-times I stand in the mid-dle of the floor,

Not go - ing left, Not go - ing right. I dim _ the lights

And think _ a-bout you, Spend sleep-less nights To think _ a-bout you, You said _ you loved

me Or were you just be-ing kind? Or am I los-ing my _

mind?

IN BUDDY'S EYES
(Buddy's There)
from *Follies*

Words and Music by
STEPHEN SONDHEIM

let - ter writ - ing And know-ing Bud - dy's there. ___ Ev - 'ry morn - ing,

(L.H.)

Don't faint, I tend the flow - ers. ___ Can you be-lieve it? Ev - 'ry week - end

I paint for ump - teen ho - urs. ___ And,

yes, I miss ___ a lot, liv - ing like ___ a shut - in. No, I have - n't got

feel like cry - ing and...

2nd time:
In Bud - dy's eyes, ———————— I'm

(Play 1st time only)

young I'm beau - ti- ful.—— In Bud - dy's eyes, ———————— I

can't get old - er.—— I'm still the prin - cess, ——

Still the prize. _____ In Bud-dy's eyes, _____

_____ I'm young, I'm beau - ti - ful. _____ In Bud-dy's arms, _____

_____ On Bud - dy's shoul - der, _____ I

won't get old - er. _____ Noth - ing dies.

DIAMONDS ARE A GIRL'S BEST FRIEND

from *Gentlemen Prefer Blondes*

Words by LEO ROBIN
Music by JULE STYNE

146

AIN'T THERE ANYONE HERE FOR LOVE?

from *Gentlemen Prefer Blondes*

Lyric by HAROLD ADAMSON
Music by HOAGY CARMICHAEL

TURN BACK, O MAN

from the musical *Godspell*

Words and Music by
STEPHEN SCHWARTZ

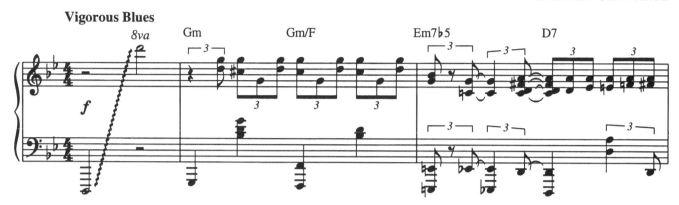

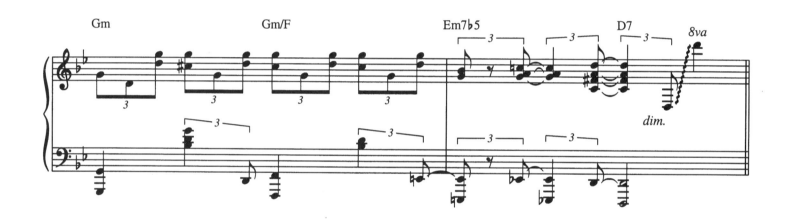

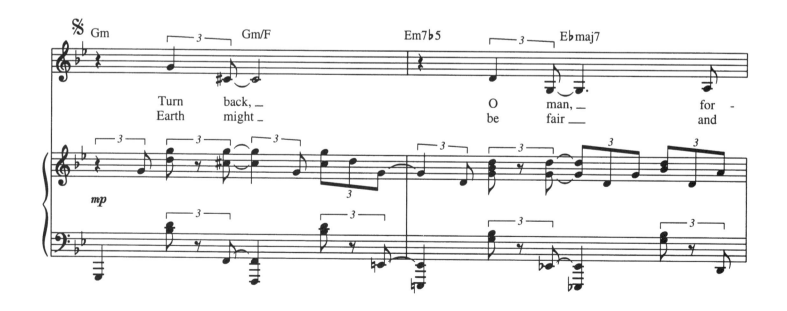

*The ad libs. (in parentheses) are merely suggestions, not necessarily the lines you will want to use.
Ad libs., when possible, should be based on the actual audience members (for instance: "Hiya, Curly" to a bald man, etc.)

swear thy _ fool - ish _ ways. _ *Spoken: See ya' later—I'm going to the front of the the-a-ter.*

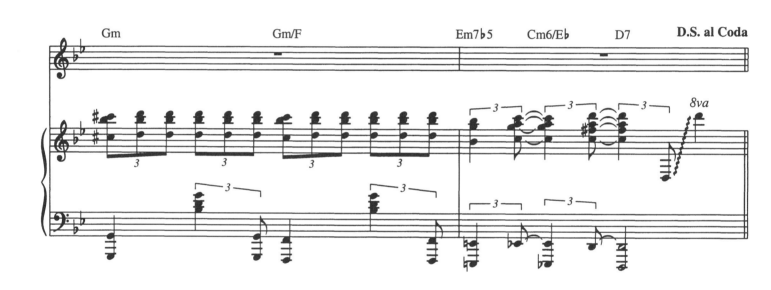

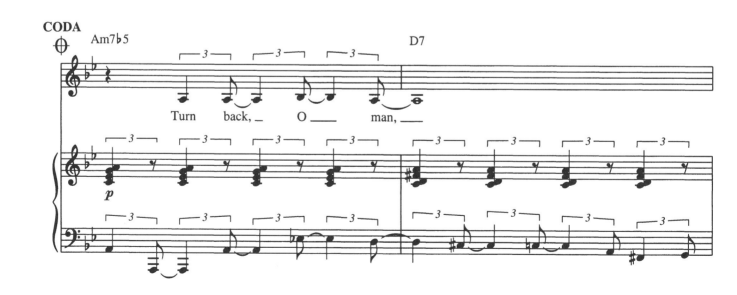

Turn back, _ O _ man, _

TAKE BACK YOUR MINK
from *Guys and Dolls*

By FRANK LOESSER

Very Slowly

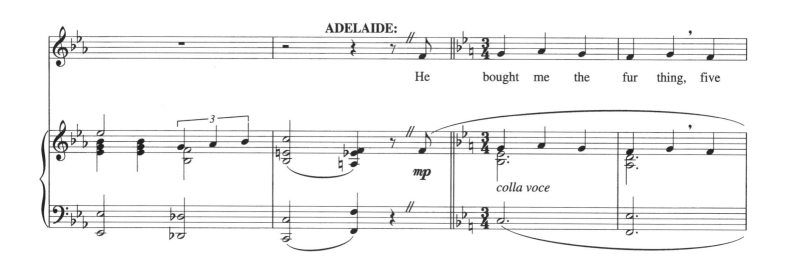

ADELAIDE:

He bought me the fur thing, five

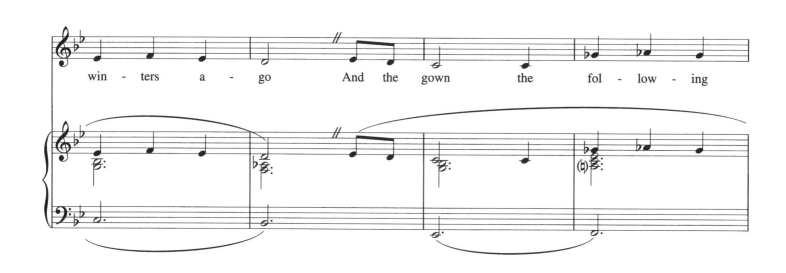

win - ters a - go And the gown the fol - low - ing

fall. _____ Then the neck - lace, the bag, the

gloves and the hat, That was late for - ty eight, I re -

suddenly
indignant

call. _____ Then last night in his a -

part - ment _____ He tried to re - move them

resentfully

all! And I said as I ran down the

rit. **Tempo di Valse** *with hurt feeling*

hall. Take back your mink

Take back your pearls what made you think That

I was one of those girls?

Take back the gown, the shoes and the hat

I may be down but I'm not flat as all that

freely

I thought that each ex - pen - sive gift you'd ar - range was a

to - ken of your es - teem. Now when I think of what you

want in ex - change, it all seems a

hor - ri - ble dream. So take back your mink To

from whence it came And tell them____ to Hol - lan - der - ize it

for some oth - er Dame.

HAPPY TO KEEP HIS DINNER WARM

from *How to Succeed in Business Without Really Trying*

By FRANK LOESSER

SOME PEOPLE

from *Gypsy*

Words by STEPHEN SONDHEIM
Music by JULE STYNE

five! _____ But I _____

at least ___ got - ta try, _____

When I ___ think of all the sights that I ___ got - ta see yet,

All the plac - es I ___ got - ta play, All the things that I ___ got - ta be yet ___

Come on, Pop-pa, whad-da-ya say? Some peo-ple can

be con-tent__ Play-ing Bing-o and

pay-ing rent.__ That's peach-y for

some peo-ple, For some hum-

won - der - ful dream, Pop - pa!

All a - bout June and the Or - phe - um cir - cuit_ Give me a chance and I

know I can work it! I had a dream,_____

Just as re - al as can be, Pop - pa!

Fl.

There I was in Mis-ter Or-phe-um's of-fice,—

And he was say-ing to me: "Rose!—

Get your-self some new___ or-ches-tra-tions, New rou-tines and red___

___ vel-vet cur-tains. Get a feath-ered hat___ for the ba-by,

Pho-to-graphs in front __ of the thea-tre. Get an a-gent

And in jig time You'll be be-ing booked __ in the big time!"

Oh, what a dream, _____ A

won-der-ful dream, Pop-pa. And

bye _____ To blue - ber - ry

pie! _____ Good rid - dance to

all the so - cials I _____ had to go to, All the lodg - es I _____

_ had to play, All the Shrin - ers I _____ said hel - lo to _

Hey, L. A., I'm com - ing your way! Some peo - ple sit

on their butts, — Got the dream,_ yeah, But

not the guts!_ That's liv - ing for some peo -

- ple, For some hum - drum peo - ple, I sup - pose.___

Well, they can stay and

rot,

mp

cresc. poco a poco al fine

But not

Rose!

sfz

WHY CAN'T YOU BEHAVE?

from *Kiss Me, Kate*

Words and Music by
COLE PORTER

Slow blues
LOIS:

Andante

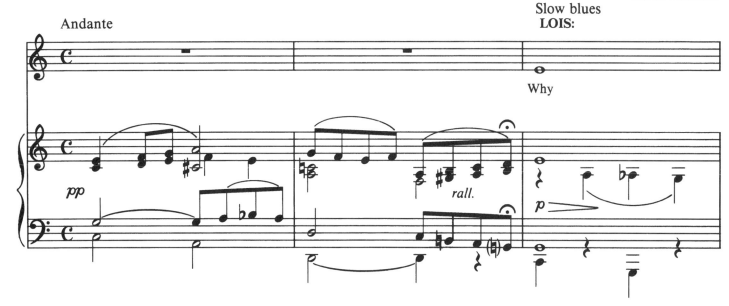

Why

can't you be - have? _____ Oh, why

can't you be - have? _____ Af - ter all the things you

Slowly

There I'll care for you for-ev - er, 'Cause you're all in the world I

a tempo

crave, But why can't you be - have? Gee, do you

need me, kid?___ I al - ways knew you did.___ But

why can't you be - have?___

8va basso

ALWAYS TRUE TO YOU
IN MY FASHION

from *Kiss Me, Kate*

Words and Music by
COLE PORTER

Oh, Bill, Why can't you be - have? ___

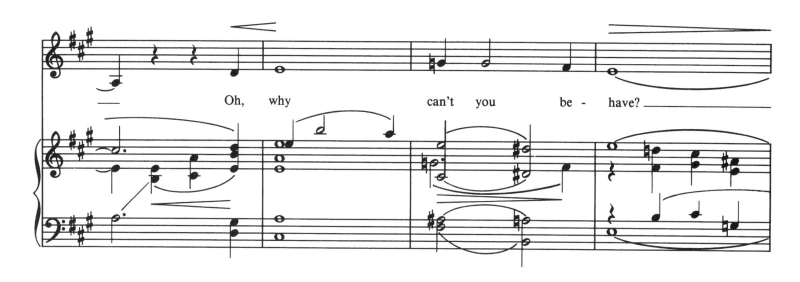

Oh, why can't you be - have? ___

How in hell can you be jeal - ous ___ When you know, ba - by, I'm your

slave?   I'm just mad for you, And I'll   al - ways be, But   nat - ur - al - ly,___

Medium bounce

If a   cus - tom tail - ored vet___ Asks   me   out for some - thing wet,___
asked   to   have   a   meal___ By   a   big   ty - coon   in steel,___

When   the   vet   be - gins   to   pet,___ I   cry "hoo - ray!"___
If   the   meal   in - cludes   a   deal,___ ac - cept   I   may!___

But I'm   al - ways   true   to you,___ dar - lin', in my fash - ion,

Yes, I'm al-ways true to you, ___ dar-lin' in my way. ___

I en-joy a ten-der pass ___ By the boss of Bos-ton
I could nev-er curl my lip ___ To a dazz-lin' dia-mond

Mass. Though his pass is mid-dle class ___ and not "Back Bay!" ___
clip, Though the clip meant "let 'er rip" ___ I'd not say "Nay!" ___

But I'm al-ways true to you, ___ dar-lin' in my fash - ion.

THE MILLER'S SON

from *A Little Night Music*

Music and Lyrics by
STEPHEN SONDHEIM

mouths to be fed And a lot in be - tween in the mean - while._____

_____ And a girl ought to cel - e - brate what pass - es

Tempo I   Rubato

by.   Or I shall mar - ry the bus'-ness - man,

Five fat ba - bies and lots of se - cur-i-ty.   Fri - day nights, if we

think we can, We'll go danc-ing. Mean-while... It's a

push and a fum-ble and a tum-ble in the sheets And I'll foot the high-land

fan - cy, _____ A dip in the but-ter and a flut-ter with what meets my

eye. _____ It's a

tas - tic, _____ With flings of con - fet - ti and my pet - ti - coats a - way up

high. _____ It's a

ver - y short way from the fling that's for fun To the

thigh press - ing un - der the ta - ble. _____ It's a

man-y a bed, There's a lot I'll have missed But I'll not have been

dead when I die! _____ And a per-son should

cel - e - brate ev - 'ry - thing _____ pass - ing

[Tempo I]

rit.

by. _____ And I shall mar-ry the mil-ler's_ son. _____

SEND IN THE CLOWNS
from *A Little Night Music*

Music and Lyrics by
STEPHEN SONDHEIM

prove? One who keeps tear-ing a-round, One who can't move. Where are the

clowns? Send in the clowns. Just when I'd stopped o-pen-ing

doors, Fi - nal -ly know-ing the one that I want - ed was

yours, Mak-ing my en-trance a-gain with my u-su-al flair, Sure of my

Is-n't it rich, Is-n't it queer, Los-ing my

tim-ing this late in my ca - reer? And where are the clowns? There ought to be

clowns. Well, may-be next year. . .

I CAIN'T SAY NO

from *Oklahoma!*

Lyrics by OSCAR HAMMERSTEIN II
Music by RICHARD RODGERS

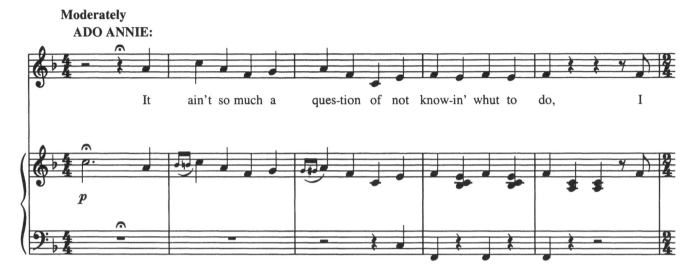

It ain't so much a ques-tion of not know-in' whut to do, I

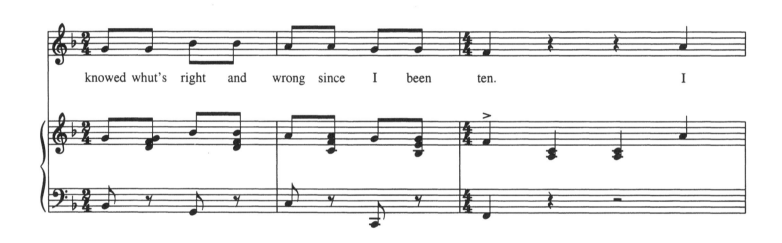

knowed whut's right and wrong since I been ten. I

heared a lot of sto-ries and I reck-on they are true A-

bout how girls 're put up-on by men.   I

know I mus-n't fall in-to the pit, _____ But when I'm with a fel-ler, I fer-

git!

f   *dim.*

mp

I'm jist   a   girl   who   cain't   say   no,
I'm jist   a   girl   who   cain't   say   no,

I'm in a tur-ri-ble fix _____
Cain't seem to say it at all _____

I al-ways say, "Come on, le's go,"
I hate to dis-ser-point a beau

Jist when I or-ta say "nix!" _____ When a
When he is pay-in' a call. _____ Fer a

per-son tries to kiss a girl, I
while I ack re-fined and cool, A-

I cain't be pris-sy and quaint
In a som-bre-ro and chaps

I ain't the type that c'n faint
Soon as I sit on their laps

cresc.

How c'n I be whut I ain't? I
Sump-'n in-side o' me snaps! I

cain't say
cain't say

HE WASN'T YOU

from *On a Clear Day You Can See Forever*

Words by ALAN JAY LERNER
Music by BURTON LANE

What could I do? He was-n't you.

rubato He was-n't you and no vows ev-er chained me. No,

he was-n't you and good-byes nev-er pained me.

Now I know Why ev-'ry hope al-ways fad-ed so

fast: _____ On - ly with you was I born to live;

On - ly to you have I love to give, Love that for all of a life - time will

last.

WHAT DID I HAVE THAT I DON'T HAVE?

from *On a Clear Day You Can See Forever*

Words by ALAN JAY LERNER
Music by BURTON LANE

great big lack of? Some-thing in me then He could see then

Beck-ons to him no more. I'm

Just a vic - tim of time, Ob - so - lete in my

prime! Out of date and out - classed

I'm not like? What was the charm that I've run dry of?

What would I give if my old know - how still knew

how! Oh! What did I have I

don't have now?

A COCKEYED OPTIMIST

from *South Pacific*

Words by OSCAR HAMMERSTEIN II
Music by RICHARD RODGERS

cur - a - bly green! I have heard peo-ple rant and rave and bel - low That we're done and we might as well be dead But I'm on - ly a cock - eyed op - ti - mist And I can't get it in - to my head. I hear the hu - man

tel - li - gent and smart _____ But I'm stuck (like a dope!) with a

thing called hope, And I can't get it out of my heart. _____

poco a poco cresc.

Not _____ this _____ heart. _____

(mf)

I'M IN LOVE WITH A WONDERFUL GUY

from *South Pacific*

Words by OSCAR HAMMERSTEIN II
Music by RICHARD RODGERS

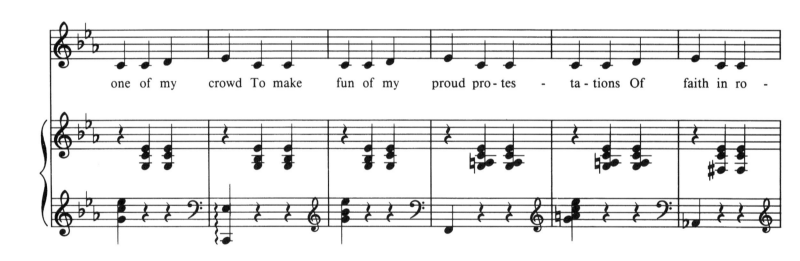

And they'll say I'm na - ive As a babe to be - lieve An - y

fa - ble I hear from a per - son in pants

Fear - less - ly I'll face them and ar - gue their doubts a - way

Loud - ly I'll sing a - bout flow-ers and spring

Flat - ly I'll stand on my

lit - tle flat feet and say Love is a

grand and a beau - ti - ful thing.

I'm not a-shamed to re - veal

The world fa - mous feel - ing I feel

Refrain

I'm as corn - y as Kan - sas in

Au - gust, I'm as nor - mal as blue - ber - ry pie, No more a

smart lit-tle girl with no heart, I have found me a won-der-ful guy!

I am in a con-ven-tion-al dith-er With a con-

ven-tion-al star in my eye, And you will note There's a lump in my

throat When I speak of that won-der-ful guy! I'm as trite and as

gay As a dai-sy in May, A cli-che com-ing true!

I'm bro-mid-ic and bright As a moon-hap-py night Pour-ing light on the

dew! I'm as corn-y as Kan-sas in Au - gust,

High as a flag of the fourth of Ju - ly! If you'll ex-cuse an ex -

pres - sion I use, I'm in love, I'm in love, I'm in love, I'm in love, I'm in

love with a won - der - ful guy!

I'm as corn - y as Kan - sas in Au - gust, High as a flag on the

fourth of Ju - ly. If you'll ex - cuse an ex - pres - sion I use, I'm in

love, I'm in love, I'm in love, I'm in love, I'm in love, I'm in love, I'm in

poco a poco cresc.

love, I'm in love, I'm in love, I'm in love, I'm in love, I'm in love, I'm in love, I'm in

love, I'm in love, I'm in love, I'm in love with a won - der - ful guy!

ff   *sf*

BY THE SEA

from *Sweeney Todd*

Lyrics and Music by
STEPHEN SONDHEIM

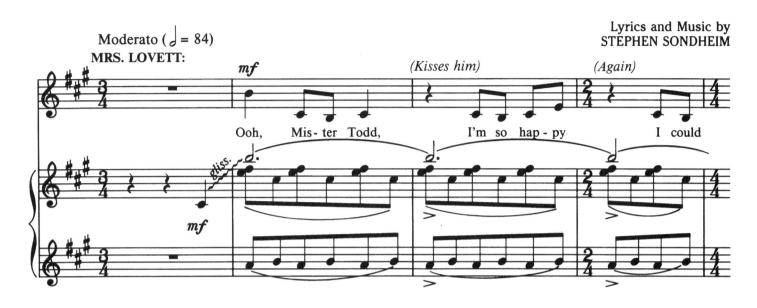

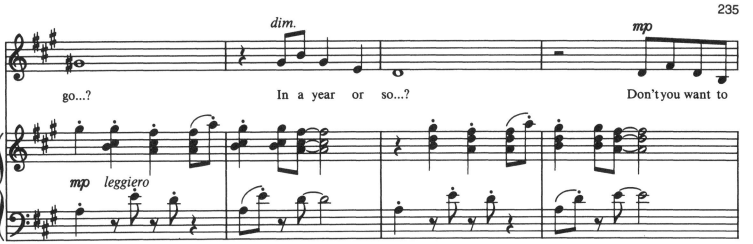

go...?　In a year or so...?　Don't you want to

know?　Do you real-ly want to know?

(Settling back) I've always had a dream -- ever since I was a
skinny little slip of a thing and my rich Aunt Nettie used to
take me to the seaside August Bank Holiday...the pier...
making little castles in the sand. I can still feel me toes wig-
gling around in the briny.

(last time)

By the

see us wak-ing, The break-ers break-ing, The sea-gulls squawk-ing, Hoo! Hoo! I do me bak-ing, Then

(sempre leggiero)

mp   L.H. *p*   *mp*

(Waving gaily)

I go walk-ing with you - hoo! Yoo - hoo! I'll warm me bones on the es - pla - nade, Have

L.H.

tea and scones with me gay young blade, Then I'll knit a sweat -er while you write a let-ter, Un-

(Coyly)

less we got bet - ter to do - hoo.   Think how

sea - side, Hoo! Hoo! By the beau-ti-ful sea! _____

Oh, I can see us now -- in our bathing dresses -- **Moderato** you in a nice rich navy -- and me, stripes perhaps.

mp

mf

p

It - 'll be so qui-et that who'll come by it Ex-

dim. poco a poco

p

cept a sea-gull? Hoo! Hoo! We should-n't try it, Though, till it's le-gal For two-hoo!

L.H.

guest to rest _ in.. Now and then, you could do the guest _ in.. By the sea,

Mar- ried nice and prop - er, _____ By the sea.

(Slashes

Bring a - long your chop - per _____ To the sea - side, Hoo!

the air twice)

Hoo! By the beau - ti - ful sea! _____

THE WORST PIES IN LONDON

from *Sweeney Todd*

Lyrics and Music by
STEPHEN SONDHEIM

244

(Plucks some-
thing off a pie)

(Drops it
on the (Stomps
floor) on it)

head's a lit-tle vague. Ugh! What is that? But you'd think we had the plague from the way that peo-ple

(Flicks at some-
thing on the
counter)

(Spots it
moving)

(Smacks it
with her hand)

(Looks at
her hand)

(Wipes it on
her apron)

keep a-void-ing...No, you don't! Heav-en knows I try, sir! Yich! But there's no-one comes in

(Blows dust off
the pie as she
brings it to him)

e-ven to in-hale. Tsk! Right you are, sir, would you like a drop of ale? Mind you, I can hard-ly

poco rit.

Meno mosso, sempre rubato

14   *sempre f*

blame them.   These are prob-a-bly the worst pies in Lon-don.

*L.H./
mf poco rit.*

mp espressivo

mf

cresc.

I know why no-bod-y cares to take them. I should know, I make them, But good? No, The worst pies in Lon-don.

E - ven that's po - lite. The worst pies in Lon - don.

If you doubt it, take a bite: Is that just dis-gust-ing? You have to con-

246

pie shop, Does a bus-'ness, but I no-tice some-thing weird: Late-ly all her neigh-bors'

mp *< f mp* *< f mp*

(Rolls the dough)

cats have dis-ap-peared. Have to hand it to her. *(grunt)* Wot I calls *(grunt)* en-ter-prise,

< f mf *< f mf f mf*

(Pounds the dough)

(grunt) Pop-ping pussies in-to pies. Would-n't do in my shop. Just the thought of it's e-

f mf *< f mf* *< f mf*

(Again) *rit.* - - - - - - - - - - - - - - - -

nough to make you sick. And I'm tell-ing you, them pus-sy-cats is quick. No de-ny-ing, times is

< f mf rit. - - - - - - - - - - - - *< f mf*

mf

248

I AIN'T DOWN YET

from *The Unsinkable Molly Brown*

By MEREDITH WILLSON

Allegro vigoroso

MOLLY:

Now look - a here— I am im - por - tant to me! I ain't no

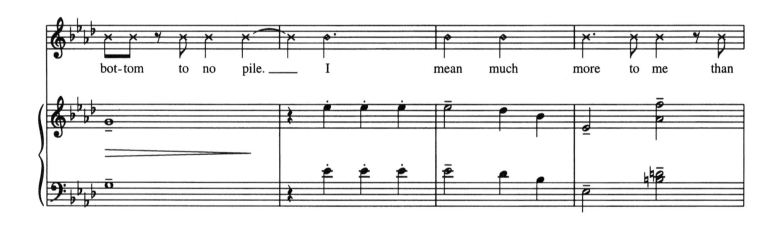

bot - tom to no pile. ___ I mean much more to me than

I mean to an - y - bod - y I ev - er knew! Cer - tain - ly more than I mean to an - y si - wash

think so. There he goes! And you can be pos - i - tive

sure I'm as good as an - y piss-ant that ev - er lived! Oh! I hate that word "Down" but I

love the word "Up," 'Cause "Up" means hope an' that's just what I got.

Hope for some place bet-ter, Some place— I dun-no— clean-er... shin-i-er...

Hell, if I got-ta eat cat-fish heads all my life, Can't I have 'em of-fa plate once?

And a red silk dress, When there's girl e-nough on me to wear one. And

then some - day, with all my

might and all my main, I'm goan' to

March

learn to read and write. I'm goan' to

see what there is to see._____ So, if you

go from no - where on the road to some-where And you

meet an - y - one, you'll know it's me. I'm goan' to

AN OLD MAN

from *Two by Two*

Words by MARTIN CHARNIN
Music by RICHARD RODGERS

Slowly - in 3

ESTHER:

An old man is queer in his

ways, His ap-pe-tite fails, But he's hun-gry for praise, And the